HINDUS
IN BRITAIN

Fiona Macdonald

Consultant: Ishwer Tailor MBE

Photography by Chris Fairclough

FRANKLIN WATTS
LONDON • SYDNEY

First published in 2005 by
Franklin Watts
96 Leonard Street
London
EC2A 4XD

Franklin Watts Australia
45-51 Huntley Street
Alexandria
NSW 2015

A CIP catalogue record for this book
is available from the British Library.
Dewey classification: 305.6'945'041

Planning and production by Discovery Books Limited
Editor: Kate Taylor
Designer: Rob Norridge

The author, packager and publisher would like to thank the
following people for their participation in this book: The Parekh
family, the Gujarat Hindu Society, Discount Auto Spares and CB
Jewellers Ltd

Photo acknowledgements: P.6 (top and bottom), Getty Images;
P.7, Hulton-Deutsch Collection/Corbis; P.16, the Parekh family;
P.26, Hulton-Deutsch Collection/Corbis; P.27, Getty Images. All
others supplied by Chris Fairclough

ISBN: 0 7496 5885 1

Printed in Dubai

Contents

British and Hindu

Around 560,000 Hindu men, women and children live in Britain today. They make up just over 1 per cent of the British population and contribute greatly to British life.

Although all Hindu people in Britain share the same faith, they do not all live in the same way. Some are rich, some are active in public affairs, some live quietly and privately and some are poor. Of Britain's 500 most wealthy families, 15 are Hindu. There are Hindu doctors and nurses, Hindu finance experts and lawyers, Hindu politicians and community campaigners – and thousands of Hindu people doing jobs in shops, offices and public service industries. Hindus also star in British films like *East is East* and popular TV sitcoms such as *The Kumars at Number 42*.

Britain's Hindu community has helped turn the country into the vibrant multicultural society it is today.

**Be loyal to the land where you live...
Strive ever to ennoble the country
which has given you shelter.**

*Dr Shastry, Hindu scholar, London,
quoting from Hindu scriptures.*

Links with India

Hinduism is a faith, not a racial description.
Many Hindu families have links through their
ancestors with the Indian subcontinent. Many
older Hindus were born there, and emigrated
to Britain to work or flee persecution. Most
Hindus speak Indian languages, such as
Gujarati, Punjabi or Tamil. They often cherish
traditions brought from their homeland, and
feel strong links with Hindus in India and
elsewhere.

Most young British Hindus, however, were
born in Britain. English is their first language,
they have studied at British schools and many
have never been to India. They may enjoy
traditional Hindu culture, but also like the
same multicultural music, food and fashions
as non-Hindus of the same age.

**The Gujarat Hindu Society's splendid
building stands prominent in the
Preston community. It is used by
people of all faiths as a community
and learning centre as well as a
temple for local Hindus.**

Ethnic mix

In the late 20th century, Hinduism attracted many Western followers
who were dissatisfied with their own culture or religion. Today, the
British Hindu community includes people from Asian, European and
American backgrounds who are inspired by, or follow, the Hindu faith.

Arriving and settling

There have been contacts between Britons and Hindus for over 400 years. British merchants travelled to India to buy spices, indigo, jute and cotton, and in 1858 India became part of the British Empire.

Working for the Empire

During the Empire era, relatively small numbers of Indians came to live and work in Britain. Some went to different parts of the Empire, like East Africa. After India was granted independence in 1947 and became part of the Commonwealth, many more immigrants began to arrive in Britain.

ESCAPE FROM AFRICA

In 1971 dictator Idi Amin (right) came to power in Uganda, East Africa. He persecuted non-Africans and forced them to flee the country. Over 30,000 Ugandan Asians sought refuge in Britain. Hindus also fled to Britain from Uganda's neighbour, Kenya, fearing that they too were in danger.

Hindu children arrive in Britain, 28 February 1968, from Nairobi, Kenya.

Commonwealth immigrants

In the 1950s and 1960s Britain needed workers and encouraged Commonwealth citizens to immigrate. Many Hindu men from Gujarat (northwest India) accepted this invitation. Tamils fleeing civil war in Sri Lanka soon followed. They took low-paid jobs in British factories and once they had settled, their wives and children joined them.

Arriving in Britain

We travelled by steamer boat from Bombay to England. It took around 15 days. I came with my two children to join him [my husband]. It was very, very cold. It was snowing and I had never walked on snow before so I did fall a few times.

Mrs Nandiben Patel, who arrived in England in the early 1960s.

Away from home

Their new life was not easy. Houses, food, clothes and the colder British weather were all very different from what they had known before. Many of the newcomers faced racial discrimination in housing and jobs. Some could not speak any English. Today that is less likely to be the case. Most Hindus in Britain have lived here all their lives.

The Hindu bride and groom sit in front of a bowl of flames during their marriage service at India House in London. This photograph shows the first ever Hindu wedding to take place here, on 6 October 1956.

What is Hinduism?

Hindus in Britain, like those across the world, share an ancient faith that originated in India around 5,000 years ago. Today, it is followed by over 900 million people. Hinduism has no founder and no set of religious beliefs. It has come to be described as a way of living. Although different Hindus interpret their faith in different ways, most share certain 'core' values.

Great spirit

Hindus honour a supreme force in the universe, called 'Brahman' (meaning great spirit, or great soul). Hindus also honour many gods and goddesses. Each one shows a different element of Brahman's power. The three most important gods are Brahma (the Creator), Vishnu (the Protector) and Shiva (the Destroyer and Re-creator).

AVATARS

Gods and goddesses have different avatars (appearances). Most Hindu families have their own favourites. Krishna, a brave hero, and Ram, a good king, are both avatars of Vishnu.

Murtis (images) representing, left to right, the gods Sita, Ram, Laxman and (below left) Hanuman at a Hindu temple.

Worshippers at Hindu temples offer fruit, sweets and flowers as gifts to the gods. In return, the temple priest blesses the food for the worshippers to eat.

Death and re-birth

Hindus believe that each person has their own atman, or soul. This lives on after a person dies and is reincarnated over and over again, until the soul wins moksha (freedom) and joins Brahman. This cycle of birth, death and re-birth is called samsara and is ruled by a law called karma. According to karma, each good action helps a soul progress towards Brahman; each bad action takes it further away.

The caste system

Traditionally, Hindu society was divided into four different castes, or classes. They were Brahmins (priests), Ksatryas (nobles), Vaisyas (farmers and merchants) and Sudras (workers). In the 20th century many Hindu people in India campaigned against the caste system, regarding it as unfair. Although a person's caste is still taken into consideration, for example when choosing an appropriate partner for marriage, it is less important than it used to be, especially among young Hindus who have moved out of India.

BEING HINDU

In a 2001 survey of young Hindus in Britain:

- **93 per cent said they were happy to be Hindu.**
- **85 per cent said they thought their religion helped them lead better lives.**
- **83 per cent said that it was important for them to practise their religion.**
- **81 per cent said they visited a temple regularly.**
- **78 per cent said they prayed regularly at home.**

Festivals and shrines

Most Hindus put their faith into practice. Traditionally, this consists of behaving well, studying to seek truth and devotion (worship). Hindu worship is called puja. Hindu families worship in different ways, according to their own traditions. Most worship at a mandir, or temple, every week. There are over 150 Hindu mandirs in Britain today.

Shrines

Most Hindu families have a small shrine at home. Here they say prayers, meditate and read holy scriptures; they believe these help bring them inner peace and face life's challenges with a balanced, focused mind. The shrine is usually found in the main room downstairs and contains a murti of their favourite god or goddess. Many shops and restaurants owned by Hindus have shrines in them too.

Saying prayers in front of a shrine in a Hindu home. Hands held together is a sign of respect.

HOLI

Holi celebrations outside a community centre in Lancashire.

Holi is a joyous spring festival celebrated in early March when Hindus across Britain like to get together. One tradition is for people to chase each other around throwing brightly-coloured powder. A bonfire is also lit to cleanse the air of evil spirits. After the main celebrations a meal is shared and singing and dancing takes place. People meet up outside Hindu community centres or temples, or in parks. At Rendell Park, in Leicester, around 5,000 people turn up each year to celebrate Holi. Local non-Hindus often come along to join in the festive spirit.

Community festivals

There are over 1,000 Hindu festivals in total. In Britain, the most celebrated are Navaratri, Diwali and Holi. Navaratri (Nine Nights), in September/October, celebrates the goddess Durga. Murtis of gods and goddesses are arranged outside temples and honoured by religious music, stick-dancing and story-telling. Diwali, the winter festival of lights, is the biggest celebration of all. Houses are decorated with lanterns and candles, and firecrackers are set off to welcome Lakshmi, the goddess of prosperity.

I love Holi. It's so much fun getting to throw coloured powder at each other. We get covered from head to toe and it looks so funny. Everyone is always in a good mood and even the grown-ups act like children!

Henna Parekh, Preston.

Flower petals and candles are spread out in front of a picture of Lakshmi, the goddess of wealth, to celebrate the joyful Diwali festival.

Local influences

Throughout Britain, Hindu influences have become a familiar sight. Temples and Hindu-run food shops, restaurants and businesses can be found in all major cities.

Clothes

Most British Hindus who have lived here all of their lives wear Western clothes in their day-to-day lives. They may dress up in traditional clothes for special occasions or festivals. However older women who have moved here from abroad often wear traditional saris every day. Indian clothes, bracelets and other jewellery are becoming more and more popular among non-Hindus and the influences can often be seen in new high street fashions.

SARIS

Saris are long pieces of brightly-coloured cloth that are draped around the body. Women wear them differently depending on where they are from.

Children's dress

Hindu girls wear Punjabi suits instead of saris for special occasions. Saris are too heavy and complicated for children to put on. A Punjabi suit consists of a tunic and a pair of trousers. They are often brightly coloured and decorated with sequins and patterns. Traditional dress for boys is a kurta pyjama – plain trousers and a tunic.

Local foods

Hindu-run restaurants are found throughout the UK and curries are now one of Britain's favourite meals. Chefs such as Madhur Jaffrey have become household names and Indian sauces and a variety of foods are found in most British supermarkets.

A delicious selection of Indian foods, including steamed rice, chapattis and several varieties of vegetarian curry.

Vegetarians

Most Hindus are vegetarians, believing that killing animals for food is wrong. In particular, cows are sacred. Many Hindu families prefer to eat spicy foods from the Indian subcontinent, rather than traditional British food. Food plays a big part in the everyday life of most Hindus.

Most Hindu families sit down to enjoy a traditional evening meal together.

13

A Hindu home

Hindus believe that Hinduism is a way of life, not just a belief. Because of this, homes and families are extremely important to them. Many Hindus in Britain rely strongly on their families for help, advice and support.

Traditional lifestyles

Traditionally, Hindu couples lived with other family members – usually the husband's parents. They were expected to respect and obey family elders and follow traditional male and female roles. In Britain today, it is still common to find large, extended families sharing a home.

Hindu families often live close to one another. Families usually take in relatives that have arrived from abroad, while they find work and a place of their own. It is not uncommon to find five or six houses on the same street owned by different members of the same family, and grandparents may choose to move from one child's house to another, periodically.

Hindu children spend some of their spare time at home learning more about their religion from older relatives.

This British Hindu woman works in her family's jewellery shop. Many British Hindus own their own businesses.

Hindu women

Hindu women traditionally felt pressure from in-laws to increase the family's size and status by having children quickly once they were married. They were expected to stay at home and look after the extended family.

However, almost two-thirds of Hindu families in Britain today no longer follow this traditional pattern. Husbands and wives often both have careers, and they may choose to wait before having children, or have none at all. Some young couples begin married life in their parents' home, but move out as soon as they can afford to. Others set up independent homes of their own when they wed.

It can be hard being a Hindu woman. Many are treated as second-class citizens and expected to stay indoors. I am lucky and married a man who believes I am equal to him. I help him run his business and am respected by the rest of my community. My mother thinks I should be at home all day but she is from India where that is more common. She doesn't understand the changes that are happening here.

Laxmi Joshi, London.

Childhood and growing up

In Hindu belief there are four stages of life, called ashramas, each of which has its own special duties. The first, 'student', is a time when young people learn. It is followed by 'householder', when adults must work. The third is 'retiring from work', a time for prayer and meditation and the last is 'giving up worldly things', when the soul finds freedom.

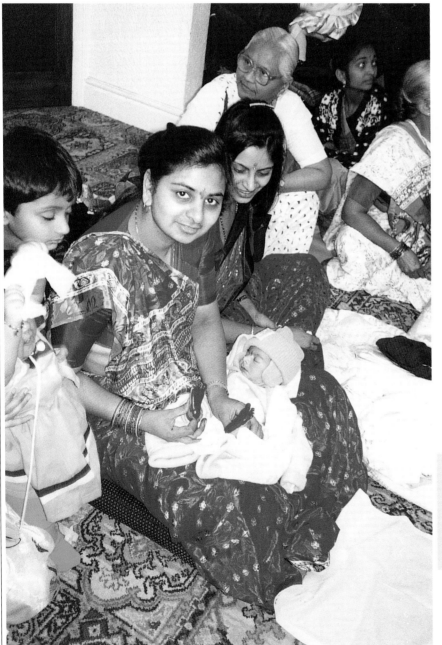

A new baby

Hindu children are welcomed as 'blessings sent by God'. Traditionally, boys were thought to be more important. They would carry on the family name and support parents in old age. In Britain's Hindu communities today, the births of boys and girls are usually greeted with equal joy. Relatives from India often make special journeys over to Britain to share in the celebrations when a baby is born.

A mother shows her son's feet, which have been coloured red with henna in this traditional Hindu naming ceremony.

Learning for life

Education is seen as very important by most Hindus. Older British Hindus see how it has helped fellow immigrants win respect and have successful careers. Hindu parents usually send children to local schools, and many pay for extra lessons from private tutors. As a result of this dedication, Hindu boys and girls achieve some of the highest marks among all school-leavers in the UK.

Many Hindu children go to weekend classes at their local temple. There, they learn traditional art, craft, music and stories.

Faith for today?

By the time they are teenagers, some young British Hindus say they need more from their community. In 2001, a survey found that they wanted better information about their faith and heritage, and improved teaching of language skills. In August 2004, a 'Get Connected' festival was held in Leicester. It was open to children from all religious and social backgrounds. Around 12,000 people attended the event, which was designed to teach about different aspects of Hindu life.

It's really important for young people, Hindu or otherwise, to understand Hindu religion and culture. As a minority group in this country, helping people become more aware of our background will improve community understanding and give more confidence to Hindu youths throughout Britain.

Hema Lad, Organizer, Get Connected.

Weddings and funerals

In the past, Hindu parents arranged marriages for their children. They looked for partners with good character, prospects and from the same caste. Girls' parents were expected to provide a dowry (goods or money for the bridegroom's family). Traditionally children had no choice but to marry the person their parents had chosen. Today, however, most unmarried Hindus hope to choose their own partner, who may even be from a different faith.

Wedding ceremonies

A Hindu wedding takes months of preparation. Days before, the bride and groom are massaged with turmeric (an antiseptic spice), to give their skin a lucky golden glow.

Hindu wedding ceremonies in the UK are similar in size and grandeur to those in other countries, such as India. Often large numbers of relatives come over from abroad – celebrations surrounding a wedding can last for weeks! The wedding itself may include fire rituals, prayers, singing and dancing and lots of food.

A Hindu bride and groom walk hand in hand around a sacred fire, while a priest (left, in white) chants from the Hindu scriptures.

WEDDING CLOTHES

At a Hindu wedding, the bride and groom are magnificently clothed, in lucky colours of red, pink, cream or gold. The bride's hands may be decorated with patterns in mehendi (henna). Guests also wear their best clothes. Men wear long Indian jackets and tight trousers, or smart western suits. Women and girls wear saris, or Punjabi-style tunics and trousers, plus ornate gold necklaces, bracelets and rings. Wedding jewellery can be spectacular and there are many fine jewellers around Britain catering for this demand, often importing their goods from India.

An elaborate gold necklace. After a wedding, many Hindu women wear simpler gold chains to show that they are married.

Earth and fire

Hindus believe in reincarnation – that when a person dies their soul moves from one body into the next. Hindus are never buried, but cremated, believing that burning the body of a dead person is the only way to release their spirit. Hindu funeral services take place at crematoriums throughout Britain. Following ancient tradition, British Hindus often take the ashes of dead relatives to India, to scatter them on the holy River Ganges.

Focus on Preston

The first Hindu migrants came from Gujarat to Preston, in northwest England, in the 1960s. They found work in local textile mills, and opened shops selling Indian foods and clothes. After 1970, Gujaratis were joined by Hindus from East Africa. At the last census (2001) Preston was home to 3,370 Hindus, 2.6 per cent of the city's population.

Preston today

Today, most Hindus living in Preston have been born and brought up there. They organise the yearly Preston Mela (fair) and members of the Preston Faith Forum join in community projects with people of different beliefs. In 2003, when white racists attacked Preston's ethnic minorities, the Forum worked hard to restore good inter-community relationships.

Most of the Hindu families around Preston chose to live in the same two or three areas. They are often on the same road as other family members. However, they also have friendly bonds with non-Hindu Britons.

Stalls selling cloth (some imported from India) at a weekly market in Preston. Local Hindu women often buy material here to make their traditional outfits.

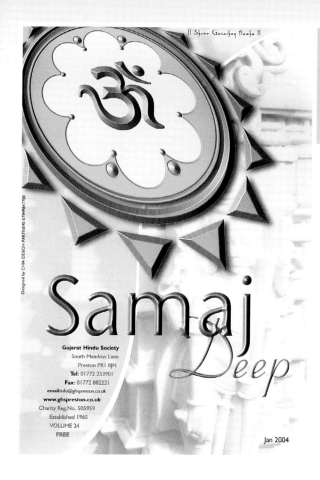

Designed by CHIA DESIGN PARTNERS 07949647750

|| Shree Ganeshay Namha ||

Samaj Deep

Gujarat Hindu Society
South Meadow Lane
Preston PR1 8JN
Tel: 01772 253901
Fax: 01772 882221
email:info@ghspreston.co.uk
www.ghspreston.co.uk
Charity Reg.No. 505959
Established 1965
VOLUME 24
FREE

Jan 2004

The Gujarat Hindu Society prints and publishes *Samaj Deep* – a community magazine in Gujarati, with local and Indian news that reports on cultural and social activities.

The Gujarat Hindu Society

Hindu life in Preston centres around the Gujarat Hindu Society. Its magnificent building features carved marble pillars imported from India (see page 5) and has banqueting and dining rooms. As well as being a place of worship, the Society has sports and youth clubs and gives training in new technology, welfare advice, and classes in dance, music, and the Gujarati language.

The Society is a popular meeting place where Hindus come to talk to one another about problems, beliefs, or just to chat. People who work there get help and support from local non-Hindus and the police force to create a friendly and welcoming environment for anyone who visits the Society.

Through a community effort by those past and present, mountains have been moved and our dream of having a purpose-built centre achieved. Certainly a building to be proud of, but more than this, we have provided a legacy to sustain our rich, Hindu, cultural heritage for future generations.

Ishwer Tailor MBE, JP, President of Gujarat Hindu Society, Preston.

Hindu elders enjoy meeting for lunch at Preston's Gujarat Hindu Society. Lunch is served free to them once a week, cooked and served up by volunteers.

The world of work

Working hard to support a family and a high regard for education are both Hindu ideals. For these reasons, many British Hindus have achieved great success in their careers.

Hindu workers in Britain

The first Hindus in Britain often worked in low-paid jobs. But today well-qualified Hindu people hold many top positions, and enterprising Hindus run successful businesses, small and large. Hindu professionals are respected in medicine, accountancy, pharmacy and law, and lead research in universities. Lord Desai is one of Britain's top economists and there are Hindu members of Parliament, such as Lord Dholakia, president of the Liberal Democrats.

However there are still no Hindu senior judges or top police officers in Britain. This has led to claims that ethnic and religious minorities are discriminated against by traditional institutions in Britain.

This Hindu mechanic works hard at running his own garage.

A woman tries on jewellery at this Hindu-owned shop. Glamorous Hindu style is now admired by many British women.

Women and work

Hindu tradition values women as homemakers, but many Hindu women have high-flying careers. For example, Anita Bhalla, presenter of Channel Four's *Eastern Eye* series, has won praise for 'transforming British broadcasting'. Hindus have also set up organizations to create work opportunities for women, and encourage education, training and self-confidence for all ethic minority women.

PATAK SAUCES

The Pathak family arrived in England from Kenya in 1956 with just £5 in their pockets. They settled in London, where Mr Pathak worked 18 hours a day making Indian foods in a small kitchen. Today 'Patak' brand sauces, pickles and spices can be found on most British supermarket shelves. The Pathak family company now employs 600 people, and is worth many millions of pounds.

Charity

Hinduism teaches that wealth is to be welcomed, enjoyed and shared. Many Hindus give generously to charities and political parties. They also make time for seva (voluntary work), an important part of Hindu tradition. For instance, Veena Loomba, nominated in 2003 for the prestigious Asian Women Achievers award, has raised over £600,000 to help widows and children.

Entertainments

Music, singing, chanting and dance all form part of Hindu worship and festival celebrations. Actors, dancers and storytellers often perform tales from the Ramayana, an epic poem describing the dramatic adventures of Hindu gods, heroes and demons.

Traditional music

Hindu classical music is based on chants from the Vedas (ancient Hindu holy texts). It is often very complicated and requires great skill to perform. Popular instruments are the sitar, with 19 strings, and the tabla, drums played with the fingers. Hindu temple musicians can also be heard playing the harmonium (a type of keyboard). Performers from India regularly come over to major cities in Britain to put on shows that are enjoyed by people from all religious backgrounds.

Hindu musicians play the harmonium (left) and the tabla (right) – two traditional Indian instruments used in many festivals and celebrations.

Dancing

Traditional dancers wear elaborate clothes and jewellery, and, sometimes, bells around their ankles that make patterns of sound as they move. Dancing is one of the favourite hobbies for young girls and boys in Britain and after-school and weekend classes are held in cities throughout the UK. More recently performers have been experimenting with fusion styles blending Indian and Western traditions, such as bhangra and chutney.

The big screen

Bollywood is the largest film industry in the world and its films are popular with people of all ages. Made in the Indian city of Mumbai (Bombay), they feature glamorous actors, lavish costumes, singing, dancing and exciting plots. Some British cinema chains have started to show Bollywood films in areas with large Hindu populations. Hindu-run shops sell countless Bollywood DVDs, videos and CDs, and glamorous posters of favourite stars can be seen in their shop windows.

Videos of Bollywood movies are very popular with customers at this Indian-run local store.

Hindu actors and musicians can also be seen and heard on British radio and TV. Some programmes are designed for speakers of Indian languages, others, in British, appeal to a nationwide audience. Comedy show *Goodness Gracious Me*, starring Hindu actress and writer Meera Syal, made history by satirising false ideas held by British people about Hindus and other minorities.

A whole new generation of artists is coming and making itself felt... Not so much [with] traditional arts but what the local Indian generation is producing in terms of modern fusion.

Girish Karnad, Director of the Nehru Cultural Centre in London.

Not only are Bollywood films popular, but people also enjoy the music that they feature.

Threats and tensions

Like other minorities in Britain, Hindus face discrimination. Temples and shops have been firebombed or daubed with racist slogans and individuals have been harmed by lies, insults and violent attacks.

Extremism

Government laws make racial discrimination illegal, but prejudiced people still make their views clear. In 2003, for example, white political extremists attacked religious and ethnic minorities in the north of Britain; many Hindu shops were burnt in the riots that followed.

Misunderstanding

British Hindus can be insulted by ignorance and misunderstanding. Sometimes the people causing them distress often have no wish to offend, and express surprise when Hindus become annoyed. For example, one London company stamped the sacred Hindu symbol Om on slippers; another printed images of the god Krishna on bikinis. Footballer David Beckham commissioned an Indian-style portrait of himself as the Hindu god Shiva and his wife as the goddess Parvati.

Hindus protesting against racial discrimination in Britain in 1952. Protesters complained that no-one would offer them jobs.

A member of the National Front is arrested during protests in London, 2004. Racist organisations like the National Front can be a real threat to Hindus, and indeed all Asians, across Britain.

Politics

There are also tensions within the Hindu community – mostly caused by political differences. Some British Hindus take a keen interest in Indian politics, and support rival political parties there. Others fear that Hindu extremists from India will bring violent opinions to Britain, and cause problems here. In 2002, there were clashes between British Hindus and Muslims, after Indian Muslims massacred Hindu pilgrims in Gujarat.

AMRUT

In 2002, British-Indian businessman Rakshit Jagdale announced plans to sell a new brand of whisky, named 'Amrut'. According to Hindu scriptures, Amrut is the sacred nectar drunk by Hindu gods. Many Hindus do not drink alcohol and were offended. However Mr Jagdale did not see the need to apologize. 'This is an exciting market...' he said.

Future hopes and fears

British Hindus pride themselves on their hard-working, law-abiding history. As a community they have higher rates of employment and lower rates of crime than almost all other Britons. Yet, as people who have their own separate traditions from other groups within British society, they are sometimes misunderstood.

Times are changing

Hindus also have different opinions on how they should live in Britain. Some feel they want to become completely absorbed in British culture; others believe that Hindus should keep their own faith, culture and languages alive. There are also differences of opinion between generations. Young Hindus, born and bred in Britain, do not always agree with their parents about standards of behaviour, personal independence and freedom to choose their own way of life.

Cultures combine. People from all backgrounds enjoy Indian delicacies from this Hindu-run food shop.

28

Hindu communities

A 'community' has been defined as 'a group of people who share the same interests, and feel solidarity with one another'. Britain is home to many communities. Some are based on wealth or poverty; some on employment or education. Others have roots in the place where people live – such as a big city neighbourhood, or remote countryside. Some communities are based on ethnic origins or inherited social status and some on political ideas or respect for religion.

Hindu people belong to all these communities – and more. Like other men, women and children living in Britain, they belong to a wider community of British citizens. They live in British houses, pay British taxes and obey British laws. They are also members of the global community. Along with almost everyone else in the world today, they share the same fears – about violence, terrorism and environmental disaster – and the same hopes for peaceful, productive lives for themselves and their families.

The best way we can 'be British' ... is by gaining inspiration from our eternal principled Hindu values, and retaining our culture in the Western world.

Nishma Shah, Vice-president of Hindu Students' Forum UK.

Hindu children in their local park playing football, the favourite sport of all British communities.

Glossary

caste one of four social classes into which Hindu society is traditionally divided

chapatti a thin, round bread used in Indian cooking

civil war a war between different groups within the same country

Commonwealth an association consisting of Britain and states that were former British colonies, or ruled by Britain

dictator a leader who rules a country with total power and usually by force

emigrate to leave one country for another

empire a group of nations or peoples ruled by one authority

ethnic belonging to a group through descent or culture

extremist somebody holding extreme political or religious beliefs

immigrant somebody who has moved to a country to live permanently

Indian subcontinent the region in southern Asia made up from the countries of Bangladesh, India, Pakistan and Sri Lanka

meditate to empty the mind of thoughts or to think about something calmly, while relaxing

merchant somebody who buys and sells goods

multicultural the mixing of cultures of different countries, ethnic groups or religions

murti an image of a Hindu god or goddess used in worship

Muslim somebody who follows the religion of Islam

naming ceremony a ceremony where a Hindu child is officially given their name and welcomed into the world

persecution the cruel or unfair treatment of a group of people, often because of their ethnic origin or religious beliefs

public affairs issues that affect the public, usually connected to their relationship with the government

racial discrimination to treat people differently to others because of their race

racist prejudiced towards people from certain races

reincarnation the belief that a soul returns to live another life in a new body after death

ritual a procedure followed regularly and precisely, usually for religious purposes

sacred dedicated to a religious purpose

sari a traditional garment worn by women in or from the Indian subcontinent, consisting of a length of fabric wrapped around the body

shrine a place of worship

solidarity harmony of interests within a group

Further information

This is a selection of websites that may be useful for finding out further information on Hinduism and Hindus in Britain.

www.sln.org.uk/storyboard/l3.htm
  Traditional Hindu tales

www.btinternet.com/~vivekananda/
  schools1.htm
  General resources prepared by the London Hindu centre, with links

http://atschool.eduweb.co.uk/manorlh/
  hinduism/hindui.html
  A good site for children aged between 7–11, with links

www.strath.ac.uk/Departments/SocialStudies/
  RE/Database/Graphics/Artefacts/
  HAfacts.html Hindu arts and objects explained

www.bbc.co.uk/religion/religions/hinduism/
  Information about Hindu faith and practices

www.bbc.co.uk/london/yourlondon/unitedcol
  ours/hinduism/welcome_history.shtml
  A site about Hinduism in London

www.redhotcurry.com/news/hfb_launch.htm
  Lively news website aimed at Asians in Britain, with information on music, sport, food, celebrities, etc

www.hinduyouthuk.org
  A site of an organisation that aims to bring inspiring, entertaining and educational opportunities to Britain's youth

Note to parents and teachers

Every effort has been made by the Publishers to ensure that these websites are suitable for children, that they are of the highest educational value, and that they contain no inappropriate or offensive material. However, because of the nature of the Internet, it is impossible to guarantee that the contents of these sites will not be altered. We strongly advise that Internet access is supervised by a responsible adult.

Index